Using Drama to Support Literacy

Activities for Children Aged 7 to 14

John Goodwin

Paul Chapman Publishing

© John Goodwin, 2006

Illustrations © Chris Walker

First published 2006

Paul Chapman Publishing
A SAGE Publications Company
1 Oliver's Yard
55 City Road
London EC1Y 1SP

SAGE Publications Inc
2455 Teller Road
Thousand Oaks, California 91320

SAGE Publications India Pvt Ltd
B-42, Panchsheel Enclave
Post Box 4109
New Delhi 110 017

Library of Congress Control Number: 2005910368

A catalogue record for this book is available from the British Library

ISBN-10: 1-4129-2050-7   ISBN-13: 978-1-4129-2050-6
ISBN-10: 1-4129-2051-5   ISBN-13: 978-1-4129-2051-3(pbk)

Typeset by Pantek Arts Ltd, Maidstone, Kent
Printed in Great Britain by Cromwell Press Ltd, Trowbridge, Wiltshire
Printed on paper from sustainable resources

THE UNIVERSITY OF
WINCHESTER

Using Drama to Support Literacy

Contents

Foreword

Effective progress in children's writing has been an overriding concern for all primary and secondary schools. Children who find it difficult to express their thinking in writing are placed at a serious disadvantage in their educational progress. By contrast, children who write well and with confidence are able to express and develop their thinking more effectively.

The key question is, how do we teach more of our children to engage with writing to do this? The National Literacy Strategy has had a very positive effect in supporting teachers' work in the classroom and in raising standards. But all would agree that the Framework for Teaching excludes some very important experiences and approaches to the teaching and development of writing.

The power of drama provides a real context for narrative writing, and in this book the tool kit of drama strategies has been laid out and used effectively by teachers across a wider range of imaginary contexts. Using drama makes possible a vast range of themes and story contexts which enthuse and hook children into the writing process. The real dilemmas and feelings in life can all be experienced in the safe world of drama and story and together these make a perfect vehicle for developing children's writing.

Through his effective work in classrooms, John Goodwin shows that drama strategies provide an essential element in the successful teaching of writing. The pages of this book give practical support and guidance in achieving this aim.

Stephen Noon
Headteacher
St Saviour's Primary School, Isle of Wight

Acknowledgements

During the last three years the Writing through Drama Programme has been operating in Isle of Wight primary and middle schools. This publication has come about as a result of the programme and attempts to disseminate some of its exciting practice. I'd like to thank the following teachers and education staff for all their generous help in providing support, time, ideas and text:

Kevin Apps, Lorraine Armstrong, Karen Bartlett, Peta East, Amanda Johnston, Vicki Jones, Helen Lambert, Wendy Mills, Stephen Noon, Karen Osborn, Denise Stephens, Liz van Wyck, Diane Walsh, Nicky Woodford.

Special thanks to these children for permission to include their work:

John Blake
Rebecca Clawson
Rhea Elliott
Catherine Farmer
Katie Hayles
Sarah Haskin
Georgina Merryweather
Sam Miselbach
Tia Pennant-Lewis
Christie Reed
Jess Rowden
Lucy Smith
Rebecca Woodford
Gold and Platinum classes of St John's C of E Primary School, Sandown CE Primary, Isle of Wight

Acknowledgement should also be made of Ros Wilson's *Assessment Criteria*.

About the author

John Goodwin has combined teaching and writing for a number of years. After teaching drama in a mining community he became Senior Lecturer at the University of Portsmouth. More recently John has limited his university work to a part-time post and found more time for his own writing. He has written over thirty BBC Radio plays and a similar number of books for children.

Nice One Sam was published by Oxford University Press in 2002 followed by several books for struggling readers for Hodder Livewire, including the *Survivors* series in 2005 and *Water Eyes* and *Rock Stars* in 2006. His picture book *An Arkful of Animal Stories*, exploring the animal's view of Noah's Ark is to be published by Lion Hudson in 2006. John is presently writing an anthology of Christmas stories which is also to be published by Lion Hudson in 2007.

Setting the scene for this book

The room is silent. Not a muscle moves. Eyes stare and fingers are held in frozen gesticulation. Some faces are turned away as if they hadn't noticed the moment of crisis as a young child makes a bodged attempt to steal a loaf of bread in the market place. The whole class has been transported back in time over a hundred and forty years to feel what it's like to be a child living on the streets in Victorian Britain.

Later individuals speak their thoughts in role to express their emotion and feeling at the desperation of the child. The strength of feeling finds its way into individual writing which builds on the concrete experience of the drama. Children work as reporters. They conduct interviews and select quotes. They write to a tight deadline and know they must report accurately exactly what happened. The presentation of their text is enhanced by IT skills with bold headlines and later displayed on the walls of the classroom.

A Victorian workhouse matron: collaborative writing from a Year 4 class

Her eyes are crinkled.
Hands like paper.
Fish lips.
Dense dragon skin.

Black boots stomping on the ground.
Vicious stark clothes.
Power like a dinosaur
Getting closer every minute.

The scope and structure of the book

This is a practical handbook founded on work in the classroom.

Its ideas have been produced and refined by practising teachers who participated in a recent Writing through Drama Programme based on the Isle of Wight. The teachers found that drama processes raised standards of literacy in their own schools in very positive and exciting ways.

Literacy is defined here in the broadest sense: that is, as a discrete subject within the Literacy Hour and as literacy across the curriculum. Thus the book draws on lessons within the Literacy Hour and in many subject areas such as PSHE, History, Art, RE etc.

Features of the book include:

♦ A directory of drama strategies, with examples of how they are used in practice.

♦ A Lessons in Action section providing longer sequences of work.

♦ Examples of teachers' planning as a model for your own practice.

♦ Extracts of written work by children.

♦ Teacher comments in the form of journal extracts reflecting on the experience of using drama processes for the first time.

♦ A glossary of drama strategies.

EXTRACT FROM A TEACHER'S JOURNAL

The ideas started to bounce off in my mind of how I could use drama in my own teaching, to adapt it to different things I was doing. My initial reaction was to try to plan too much, to pile in loads. In practice it's been important to select a few strategies so the children and I begin to be familiar with one technique before introducing another one. Using still images has been a particular favourite and conscience alley for a drugs awareness day produced a depth of work.

The year 8s were a super cool class and I was very apprehensive before doing the lesson but it worked far better than I'd imagined. I'd been worried that some of the boys might be jokey but they were caught up in it.

Introduction
How to use this book

1. How and where do I begin to use this book?

Begin with your own ongoing work. The book is intended to dovetail with your present and future curriculum planning. Think of drama as an active learning process that will help you deliver literacy in an exciting and economic way. If you're intending to set the class a writing task with specific learning objectives then ask yourself, *Which drama strategy can I use to help the class achieve those objectives effectively?*

All strategies have the potential to increase the motivation for children to want to write.

Particular strategies help with particular areas of writing. For example hot seating helps character description. Space building will stimulate the class to focus on a sense of place in their writing.

If you're not sure about the use of individual strategies at this stage, just dip your toes in the water and try a few out. You won't be disappointed.

2. Do I need to use the school hall?

No. A cleared classroom often provides a more focused and atmospheric space than a large and booming hall. Once the class see the cleared chairs and tables or help you to clear them, *they'll be on your side and keen to make the drama work.* If your classroom is tiny ask a colleague for an exchange of classrooms and perhaps in return share the work you've achieved.

Individual clipboards, sufficient for every member of the class, are often useful for children to write on in the cleared space.

3. What's the most effective way to begin the drama?

Drama is active. Try not to talk for too long in your introduction. Work at creating an immediate tension in the drama. One basic definition of drama is: *A person in a crisis*. Allowing the class to hot seat you as a fictional character in role is an excellent way to create tension. The class will love it but you may be daunted. Be honest with the children, seek their cooperation before you begin and don't let the hot seating run for too long. Use a jacket, hat or shawl to distinguish when you're teacher and when you're in role. You may need to take a little time for the class to begin to formulate some of their questions before you step into role.

If Hot Seating is too scary a strategy at this stage find another way into the drama.

For example, still images or space building offer less risk-taking and make fewer demands on both the teacher and children. In both of these the teacher maintains a traditional role and doesn't need to step into the fiction of the drama.

4. When should the class write?

When the moment is 'hot'. The writing will be at its strongest if it comes *immediately after a drama activity* and not later that day or the following day if that's at all possible. If we've just hot seated a victim of bullying or we've created a bombed out house through a space building strategy then the richness of the experience will transfer through to our writing if the ideas are still fresh in our minds. Have individual clipboards at the ready to begin the writing immediately. Don't let yourself be carried away with an over-long sequence of drama at the expense of time for writing.

Use a range of writing techniques to follow the drama – collaborative writing with teacher as scribe, paired and individual writing as well as writing in different genres – headlines, role on the wall, letters, messages, diaries, speech bubbles etc. and non-fiction text.

Writing in role can produce exciting and powerful work.

Think about teacher as writer. A pre-written fictional diary entry can be a model of good practice as well as a strong stimulus.

5. How long should the session last?

Flexibility is key. If you're working in a primary school you may have a whole morning you can devote to this work, particularly if you're combining literacy and history or another curriculum area, for example. If you're working within the constraints of a tight timetable slot in a secondary school or with the literacy hour perhaps one drama strategy will suffice. In the plenary element of the literacy hour, for example, it would be good to use teacher in role as summation.

6. What if I wish to develop the work further?

The power of the drama and writing processes is at its most potent when they interact closely together. These are a few examples:

- Use space building to create an air raid shelter. The class sit in a confined place as if in the shelter and read extracts from their diaries.
- The class have written a message to a giant. They read it out aloud with teacher in role as the listening giant. The listening giant then reacts to the message.
- Previously written speech bubbles are added to paired still images in order to provide a snapshot play script.

The intention here is to further enhance and support the writing by giving it a fictional audience and purpose within the drama.

It's also useful to consider the unique role that drama has in slowing the moment down so we see the depth of emotion and feeling.

Using open questions as a crucial tool, the teacher can deepen the learning and reflection here rather than moving on quickly to another activity.

What children and teachers say

'It helps you feel what you write.'

'I like Drama because I like imagining to be other people and to be in different places.'

'I find it easier because you feel like you're there, as if you're the character.'

'When I do Drama, it makes me know what I'm going to do when I'm writing.'

'It makes me feel adventurous.'

'When we wrote about Tom's Midnight Garden and we closed our eyes in the hall, it made me feel relaxed.'

'It's a wonderful creation.'

'SATs are coming up soon and I must continue with the drama because it unlocks the ability to write, to use words. It helps them to think about what a writer doesn't say. Children at Yr 6 are just beginning to 'read between the lines'. The less able are taking only literal meaning perhaps but with the help of drama they are beginning to see what the writer isn't saying. Beginning to infer and speculate … all those higher order reading skills which the drama is unlocking. From that viewpoint as drama reader they can write, enabling them to get over the barrier which so many have built up. Writing has always lagged behind reading in this school and beyond. Drama links the two up in a way nothing else can.'

STRATEGIES

A tool kit for drama and a means to structure learning whatever the curriculum subject. Strategies can be used in sequences when longer time slots are available or in singles if you only have a shorter time. You don't need the hall as a cleared classroom space often is more atmospheric.

EXTRACT FROM A TEACHER'S JOURNAL

I was doing some work on the First World War poets with a year 8 class and I realised how drama could draw so much out of some difficult poetry and it worked brilliantly. We explored *Dulce et Decorum Est* through text marking, finding words that expressed tiredness, panic and disgust. By doing this we were getting into the feeling of the poem. We then created still images to show fatigue, panic and disgust. After that, working in one big circle, we used space building to create the battlefield after a gas attack and to write a description of the dereliction in 50 words. It was such powerful stuff.

CAPTION MAKING

Adding a title to a still image. Children create the title verbally or in written form. They can create a headline imagining the image as a newspaper photograph or a name if it's a painting or sculpture.

Example
History: Second World War – The Blitz

History Links:	KS2 4a, b, 5c, 8a, 11b
Literacy Links:	En1 2a, 4a, b, c, 11a; Enc3 1a, 9a, 10, 11

Activity

The drama focuses on the moment people leave the safety of an air raid shelter to discover that their house has been destroyed by bombing. They do this by creating a still image in small groups and adding their thoughts through thought tracking.

Written work

1 Ask each group to do a written version of their verbal caption.
2 Discuss these as a whole class.
3 Ask each group to write down alternative captions for their own image and/or that of other groups.

CEREMONY

Special events devised to mark, commemorate or celebrate something of cultural or historical significance.

Example
History: Saxons and Vikings

History Links:	KS2 1a, 4b, 5c, 8a, 9
Literacy Links:	En1 2a, 4a, b, c, 11a; En3 1a, b, 12

Activity

The drama focuses on a meeting between Viking invaders and Saxon settlers. A village meeting is to be held to talk over the threat of a Viking invasion which has already seen the destruction of nearby villages. Before the meeting can begin all the villagers have to take part in a simple greeting ceremony. The whole class devise the ceremony and put it into action to begin the meeting.

Written work

1 With an adult as scribe do a wholeclass written brainstorm of words and phrases that describe the village on the day of the meeting. Focus on feelings, body language and the setting of the village.

2 Openings. Working as individuals children write down their opening sentence of a description of the village at this time.

3 Having shared these as a whole class children write their own description of the village meeting in 50 words. Ask them to concentrate on the sounds, smells and sights of the village.

CONSCIENCE ALLEY

A strategy exploring tough dilemmas. A character in role walks between two rows of children (the alley). Each side offers alternative advice representing the conscience of the character. At the end of the row, the character has to make a decision based on which side was more convincing.

Example
Art and Design: Last of England

Art and Design Links:	KS2 4c, 5a
Literacy Links:	En1 2a, 4a, b, c, 11a; En3 1a, 9a, 10, 11

Activities

The class have been studying the Pre-Raphaelite painting *Last of England* by Ford Madox Brown. They imagine the two principal characters in the painting are called Robert and Sophie, who are leaving England to begin a new life in America.

The teacher or a child takes the role of either Robert or Sophie and walks down the conscience alley at the moment of decision-making about leaving England for America or staying at home. One side of the alley give reasons to stay – 'you'll never see your family again' etc., while the other side give reasons for going – 'it will be a chance for a new life' etc.

Written work

Role on the wall. Draw two outlines on paper. One is Robert and the other Sophie.

1 Half the class with the marker pens/felt tips at the ready go to Robert's outline. They choose suitable words and phrases describing how Robert feels about what he's leaving behind in England and write them out within Robert's outline.

2 The other half of the class do almost the same but go to Sophie's outline and write outside her shape her fears and feelings about what the future holds for her.

3 Then ask the groups to exchange places. The first group now focus on Sophie and repeat the task whilst the second group do the same for Robert. Once this has been completed gather everyone around the outlines and discuss the choice of phrases and words.

COSTUME OR PROP

Articles of costume or special objects presented as an introduction to a culture and lifestyle of a character or place. Alternatively decisions taken about what costume or prop would be appropriate introduced during the drama.

Example
History: Victorian Britain – The Workhouse

History Links:	1a, b, 2a, c, 4a, 8a, 11a
Literacy Links:	En1 2a, 4a, b, c, 11a; En3 2a, b, c, d, e, f

Activities

After exploring daily life in the Victorian workhouse the drama focuses on a key moment for the matron. A length of rough sacking representing a bundle wrapped round a small baby is placed on the floor at the imaginary doorway of the workhouse. This provides a concrete focus for a conscience alley strategy to decide what's to be done about the baby.

Written work

1 In 50 words write a persuasive letter urging matron to either reject or accept the baby into the workhouse.

2 Pair work. Read your letters carefully to each other and be supportive and attentive listeners. Comment on each other's writing and offer constructive advice. Choose words and phrases that are particularly effective, as well as those that might need to be reworked.

3 Redrafting. Mark your text where you need to make changes and then write a second version of your letter.

DREAM PICTURES

A whole class activity using charcoal or marker pens and a long roll of wide paper. Draw, or write words and phrases, to depict a dream which a fictional character has had. The dream may be the night before a dramatic event or at a time of crisis. The activity should express inner thoughts and feelings.

Example
Literacy: The Giant's Footprint

Literacy Links:	En1 2 b, c, 3a, b, c, f, 4a, c, 11a; En3 1a, b, 5a, b, 9a

Activities

Before the class enter the space the teacher has created the shape of a giant's big footprint on the floor. This can be done by drawing a chalk outline or placing string in the shape of the footprint.

The following activities then occur:

- Using a different space if possible, the teacher introduces the lesson by explaining that everyone is living in an imaginary land close to icy mountains. The class then moves into the space and gathers round the footprint.

- Still image and thought tracking of all inhabitants gathered round the footprint.

- Dream pictures later that night, when the identity of the footprint still isn't known. The pictures express fear and worry about what might happen next.

Written work

1 Add phrases and words to the dream pictures.

2 Create a small group still image of one moment in the dream.

3 Select words and phrases you've written down. Speaking them slowly and dramatically bring your image to life in a slow motion movement. Use repetition of words as you move slowly.

FORUM THEATRE

A situation is enacted by children assigned the established roles as the rest of the class watches. At any point and with the teacher mediating, the observers can stop the action to discuss different approaches, new developments or take time out to advise those taking the roles. Other children can also take on the roles as appropriate.

Example
PSHE and Citizenship: Breaking the Law

PSHE and Citizenship Objectives:	KS2 2b, d, f, 4a
Literacy Links:	En1 2 b, c, 3a, b, c, f, 4a, c, 11a; En2 2a, b, c, d, e, 12

Activities

Working in groups of three, the class create a still picture of someone their age shoplifting in the local corner shop. The three characters should be – the shoplifter, a friend of the shoplifter's family who sees the theft, the shopkeeper who is unaware of what happens. The action is frozen at the moment of the theft. All three are then thought tracked in order to hear their feelings and attitudes.

The dilemma of the family friend regarding possible future action is explored through forum theatre. Volunteers are asked to take the role of the family friend and one of the shoplifter's parents. The friend visits the parent and has to break the news of what they witnessed in the shop. What will they say? How is it best to approach the scene? Let the scene run and then take time out to offer advice or give opportunities for others to take the roles.

Other scenes can then be put into action, e.g. the moment when the parent confronts the thief. Should the parent be angry, aggressive, prepared to listen, firm, forgiving? Whichever attitude they take, consider if their stance will be effective in making sure that the crime does not reoccur.

 Written work

1 Choose one of the characters in the storyline and think about seeing what's happened through their eyes. Write a short monologue written from their point of view. Concentrate on their feelings and emotions.

2 Share your monologue with someone else in the class, preferably someone who has chosen a different character.

3 Select words and phrases you've written down. Speaking them slowly and dramatically bring your image to life in a slow motion movement. Use repetition of words as you move slowly.

4 Play script. Write your own scene of what happens next.

HOT SEATING

A character in role is put on the spot and questioned by the rest of the group. The character answers in role and may have an item of costume such as a shawl, cloak or hat to help them establish their fictional identity. The questioners may be in or out of role. Questions which explore feelings, relationships and motives rather than a heavy emphasis upon factual information seeking should be encouraged.

Example
RE: The Nativity – The Angel's Story

| **Literacy Links:** | QCAT 4B |

 Activities

The class have become familiar with the Nativity story and have produced their own books retelling the main events of the narrative. In order to explore different viewpoints the teacher and children take turns to hot seat one of the characters involved in the Nativity including an angel, a shepherd and even the donkey.

 Written work

1. An individual account of the Nativity seen through the eyes of one of the characters who have been hot seated.

2. Share the accounts as whole class. How and why are they different?

3. Redrafting. Having listened to other accounts return to your own and consider how your text could be written. Without copying the ideas of others, think about further detail that could be included in your own work.

JOURNEYS

A strategy for creating journeys to dangerous places, distant lands or imaginary countries. The teacher leads the class through different parts of the building asking them to believe they are going on a dangerous journey. Obstacles such as deep ravines which have to be stepped across, narrow ledges requiring single file careful foot movement, low overhanging roofs of caves where crawling is required are negotiated with or without the help of benches and carefully selected PE equipment.

Example
History: Ancient Egypt – What did Howard Carter find?

History Links:	KS2 1a, 4b, 5a, c, 13 (direct link to Ancient Egypt QCA)
Literacy Links:	En1 2a, 4a, b, c, 11a; En3 2, 9a, b, 12

Activities

The teacher explains that we are going to re-enact a true story that occurred in the Valley of the Kings in Egypt (1920).

After taking the role of Howard Carter the teacher leads the class on a journey hoping to find the lost tomb of Tutankhamun. They go down 16 steps where they pause as Howard is reluctant to break through the first door. They go through an underground passage to a second door where they look through a hole to see a chamber full of golden objects.

▶

Written work

1 Children in role as archaeologists write a report on what was found in the chamber.

2 Read some of the reports out as a whole class. Think about what a report should contain.

3 Comment on when a report is biased or mere opinion. Have you found parts of reports that are supported by evidence or facts? Why is this evidence important?

Journeys (see p.17 'Ancient Egypt – what did Howard Carter find?')

MEETINGS

Gathering together in role to discuss an issue, solve a problem or plan and agree a course of action.

Example
History: Roman Britain

History Links:	KS2 1a, b, 2a, c, d, 5a, c, 8a, 9 (direct link to Roman QCA)
Literacy Links:	En1 2b, e, 3a, c, d, f, 4a, c, 11a
PSHE and Citizenship:	KS2 2a, e, f, 4a, f

Activities

The children are in role. Half are Romans and half are Celts. Hold a meeting with teacher in role as leader of a neighbouring village where Roman occupation has already taken place. The Romans put forward positive elements that they will introduce to Celtic life. Celts express elements of their lifestyle they would like to see unchanged. Discuss and resolve, agreeing a course of action that will now occur in the Celtic village.

Written work

1 Draw up a list of combined rules for Romans and Celtic villagers to live together peacefully.

2 Work in small groups with a copy of the rules. Decide which rules are the most important. Which rules will be particularly difficult to make work?

3 Return to the roles in the drama and report back your small group discussions.

MIME

An action without words using body movement and gestures to express an idea or create a character.

Example
Literacy and Science: The Moon

Science Links:	KS2 QCA 3D, 5E
Literacy Links:	KS2 En3 1a, b, c, d, e, 2a–e, 3, 7d
Art Links:	QCA 4C

Activities

Working individually the children mime preparations for going into space. They say goodbye to friends and family, put on special clothing and heavy moon boots. Carrying their space helmets they walk slowly to the platform and climb into the spacecraft. During this activity the quality of the mime is important to build belief. They have to reach out with their arms and finger tips to put the suits on and feel the heavy weight of the boots. Walking is difficult with the boots on as is climbing into the spacecraft. Sound effects and music provide a stimulus for the space journey and for the exploration of the surface of the moon where rock samples are collected. Finding a weird footprint provides a further development of the drama, which can be extended by other strategies.

▶

Written work

1 With the teacher as scribe, and working as a whole class, write a collaborative letter to an alien.

2 Individual writing. Working as a solo activity, children write their own version of the letter, adding original words and ideas where possible. The text should be written in three paragraphs each with a clear and distinct focus.

MODELLING

Work in pairs with one a sculptor and one as a passive block of clay. The sculptor creates a statue or frozen character by moving the body of the block of clay into appropriate positions.

Example
Literacy: The Giant's Footprint

Literacy Links:	En1 2b, c, 3a, b, c, f, 4a, c, 11a

Activities

Before the class enter the space the teacher has created the shape of a giant's big footprint on the floor. This can be done by drawing a chalk outline or placing string in the shape of the footprint.

The following activities then occur:

◆ Using a different space if possible, the teacher introduces the lesson by explaining that everyone is living in an imaginary land close to icy mountains. The class then moves into the space and gathers round the footprint.

◆ Still image and thought tracking of all inhabitants gathered round the footprint.

◆ Dream pictures that night when the identity of the footprint still isn't known, expressing fear and worry about what might happen next.

◆ Hot seat a blind old wise person in the village who says that a giant lives in the mountains and it may be her or his footprint.

◆ Modelling to create imaginary figures of the giant.

▶

Written work

1 Plan a whole class message for the giant to see. What should the message look like? Decide what materials it should be written in.

2 Working in small groups create different messages using different materials, layout and ways of communicating.

3 Consider what message the giant might send back and create it in writing or in another medium.

MOVEMENT SEQUENCES

Using a series of movements, improvised or rehearsed, to explore a situation, place, feeling or event. Movement sequences can be more abstract than mime.

Example
Literacy and Science: The Moon

Science Links:	KS2 QCA 3D
Literacy Links:	KS2 En3 1a, b, c, e, 2a, b, 3, 7a, d, 12

Activities

Working as individuals the class explore the feelings of imaginary weightlessness during a space journey to the moon. A tape of appropriate sound effects may be used to support this activity.

Written work

1 Think about what a letter home might look like. Write out the opening line of the letter.

2 In pairs share your lines.

3 Write out the full letter and describe what it's like in space.

Movement Sequences (see p. 25 'The Moon')

NARRATE

To tell a story or part of a story to set the scene, offer information or move the drama on in time. The children either listen to the narration or enact it as it is spoken. There are times when children might narrate.

Example
Literacy: Exploring a Myth

Literacy Links:	En1 2b, c, 3a, b, c, f, 4a, c, 11a

Activities

The teacher introduces the class to a myth by the following narration:

Long ago and far away there were two islands in the middle of the ocean. One of the islands was large and the other very small. There is talk that there was once a third island that has long since disappeared.

The people on the two islands are very different. The smaller islanders enjoy life and take things easy. They spend much time on the beach watching the waves and feeling the warmth of the sun. All the islanders are equal and they have no ruler or chief. On windy days they fly their kites. They use the blue shells on the beach to make necklaces and bangles.

The greater islanders work from dawn until dusk every single day. They are well organised and efficient. Everyone is expected to build and dig and fish and grow crops and use blue shells as money. They have a chief who everyone has to obey.

Written work

1 Role on the wall. Split the class into two groups of lesser and greater islanders. Fill in your drawn outline with words and phrases which describe the way you see yourselves, giving details of lifestyles etc.

2 Exchange outlines and, writing on the outside of the outline, use contrasting words and phrases to describe the lifestyle of the people from the other island.

3 Take a vote – which lifestyle would you like to live? Give reasons for your choice.

ROLE ON THE WALL

Writing words and phrases which describe a character. A large sheet of paper is taped to the floor at either end of the room and a child is asked to lie down on it. While they keep very still the class draw round their outline. They then lift themselves clear of the paper. The class fill their outline with words which describe a fictional character from a book, poem or story. Shapes created in different ways can extend this activity.

Example
Geography: A Village in India

Geography Links:	QCA 10A

Activities

After hot seating teacher in role as a young girl from an Indian village, the class works in groups of four on the role on the wall strategy. Using a member of their group they create an outline of the Indian child. Inside her outline they write words and phrases to describe what possessions the child has and what her life is like. Outside the outline they then write about their own life by giving details of lifestyle and possessions. Discussion then follows of differences and similarities between the two.

Written work

1 Collaborative writing. With an adult as scribe draft a beginning of a description of the village. Choose unusual words and ideas. Remember to begin sentences in a variety of ways. Build and develop complex sentences. Challenge the class and build a model of good practice.

2 Independent writing. Children continue the description as a solo activity.

3 Take the role of the young child once more and allow the children to place their writing before you, perhaps reading out small extracts. Add a final comment of your own in role.

SEQUENCING

An active and fun strategy for deciding upon the order of scenes in a play, story or event. The teacher draws an imaginary time line in the room. One end of the line represents the beginning while the other is the end. The children have to call out the first scene and move themselves onto the line at the same time. Others join in spontaneously until the line and sequence are complete.

Example
History: Roman Britain

History Link:	KS2 1a, b, 2a, c, d, 5a, c, 8a, 9 (direct link to Roman QCA)
Literacy Links:	En1 2b, e, 3a, c, d, f, 4a, c, 11a

Activities

The children have previously explored the character of Boudicca and the Roman invasion of Britain. They use sequencing to recap the story of Boudicca's revolt in AD 20 by creating the active time line beginning with the first events in the revolt and concluding with the aftermath of her death.

Written work

1 Working in pairs together write out a time line of the sequence. Choose a clear layout.

2 Make your pair into a group of four and check out your two time lines together.

3 Write your own diary entry of a key episode in the revolt seen from the viewpoint of either a Roman or one of Boudicca's followers.

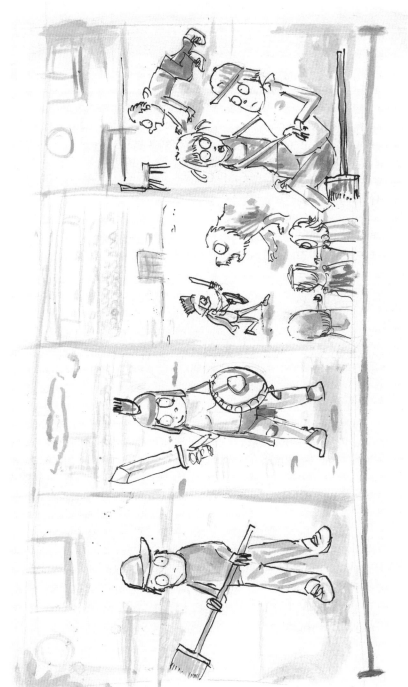

Sequencing (see p. 31 'Roman Britain')

SOUND COLLAGE

The representation of a place, mood, theme or story in sound. Instruments, the voice or objects of many kinds can be used.

Example
Art and Design: Last of England

Art and Design Links:	KS2 4c, 5a
Literacy Links:	KS2 En1 2b, c, 3a, b, c, f, 4a, c, 11a

Activities

The class have been studying the Pre-Raphaelite painting *Last of England* by Ford Madox Brown. They imagine the two principal characters in the painting are called Robert and Sophie, who are leaving England to begin a new life in America.

The class think about the journey to America and the difficulties that might be experienced. Working as a whole group a sound collage is created of a storm at sea using voices and or objects/instruments to make the sound. The teacher and children take turns to be a conductor. Individual sounds can be quietened by a wave of the hand and increased in volume by a different gesture. The collage can include thoughts and feelings of fear in addition to the sounds of the ship, sea and weather.

Written work

1 With a large sheet of paper and marker pens create a written collage of the sounds. You could do this as a whole class or in small groups.

2 Work on the computer to do a word processed version of your work. Enhance your text with different fonts and clip art.

3 Try writing your own sound poem.

SPACE BUILDING

Creating an imaginary space, environment or building by placing everyday objects to represent significant things within the space.

Example
Literacy: Narrative Writing – A Suspense Story

Learning Objectives taken from Ros Wilson's:	*Assessment Criteria Year 6 Planning and Exemplification Units*

 ### Activities

Working in small groups the class recreate rooms or areas in a 'spooky house' as they imagine them. Half the class will be recreating these as imagined by the children of the neighbourhood while the other half as seen by the old man who lives there. The group place ordinary objects to represent things or belongings. For example, a ripped newspaper represents a smashed pane of glass, an upturned hat is a bucket to catch drips from a leaky roof.

 ### Written work

1 In 50 words try and capture the room you've created.

2 Share your work with some in the class. Be good listeners and readers. Give each other feedback on your work.

3 Redraft your work in response to comments made in the pair activity. How and why has it changed?

Space Building (see p. 35 'Narrative Writing – A Suspense Story')

SPEAKING THOUGHTS

Children speak the thoughts of characters. They do this individually, one at a time and on a signal from the teacher. They may mark the significance of the thought by stepping forward, turning round or lifting their heads.

Example
Literacy: Narrative Writing – A Suspense Story

Learning Objectives taken from Ros Wilson's:	*Assessment Criteria Year 6 Planning and Exemplification Units*

 Activities

The class sit in a full circle facing outwards. They are invited to speak the thoughts of children who walk across the road from a spooky old house close to where they live. They then turn inwards and speak the contrasting thoughts of the old man who lives in the house.

 Written work

The class are working on writing a suspense story and use this activity as a basis. After exploring the drama they write:

1 The opening
2 The development of the story
3 A gripping conclusion

The writing is based on Ros Wilson's guidance of resolution and ending (see pages 55–57).

STILL IMAGE

Using the body to create a frozen picture. Children work individually, in groups or as a whole class. The picture can capture a moment in time like a photograph or be more abstract to represent a painting or sculpture.

Example
Literacy: A Big Book Story

Literacy Links:	En1 2a, 4a, b, c, 11a; En3 2, 9a, b, 12

 Activities

The class have been discussing the Big Book *Hannah* set in 18th century England. The drama focuses on Hannah's visit to a London market with her father. While there Hannah's father is wrongly accused of stealing and arrested. In groups of two or three children recreate the moment of his arrest by making a still image. This is further developed by a whole class still image of the scene in the market. They may choose to be a stall holder, passerby or Bow Street Runner but not Hannah or her father. An item of costume to represent Hannah's father is placed in the centre of the room to act as a focus before the image is built.

 Written work

1 Work as reporters. Carry out interviews with other members of the class in role as witnesses. Write down quotes. Use tape recorders to help you. Take it in turn to be witnesses and reporters.

2 Work as whole class and share some of the quotes you've noted down.

3 Working by yourself, write an individual newspaper report about the arrest, including the quotes you've gathered. Care needs to be taken in the writing of this to ensure that the report isn't influenced or affected by the personal opinion of the writer. Opinion is only allowed when it is written as a quote from those who witnessed the incident.

Still Image (see p. 38 'A Big Book Story')

TEACHER IN ROLE

The teacher takes a role in the fiction of the drama. This may be to provide an initial stimulus for the lesson or to challenge decisions or attitudes, thus deepening children's thinking and learning. It is helpful if the role creates or sustains tension.

Example
Traditional Tales: The Big Bad Wolf

Literacy Links – Year 3 Term 2 Objectives:	T2, 3, 6, 78, 10, S2, S3
PSHE/Citizenship Links:	KS2 2b, f, k

Activities

After reading the story of 'Little Red Riding Hood' the class consider if the wolf is guilty of plotting to eat grandma and Little Red Riding Hood.

With the teacher in role as the judge the children take the role of solicitors. They have to deliver their prepared statements of evidence. The judge decides if they are persuasive enough to convict the wolf of guilt.

Written work

1 Role on the wall: The class fill in an outline of the wolf with adjectives to describe his appearance and behaviour.

2 Shared writing: Opening paragraph for the prosecution when the wolf comes to trial. Why is the wolf guilty?

3 Read out your texts to the whole class.

THOUGHT TRACKING

Children speak the thoughts, feelings and emotions of characters at a given point in the drama. This is often used during or after a still image has been created.

Example
PSHE and Citizenship: Breaking the Law

PSHE and Citizenship Objectives:	KS2 2b, d, f, 4a
Literacy Links:	En1 2b, c, 3a, b, c, f, 4a, c, 11a; En2 2a, b, c, d, e, 12

Activities

Working in groups of three, the class create a still picture of someone their age shoplifting in the local corner shop. The three characters should be – the shoplifter, a friend of the shoplifter's family who sees the theft, the shopkeeper who is unaware of what happens. The action is frozen at the moment of the theft. All three are then thought tracked in order to hear their feelings and attitudes. The dilemma of the family friend regarding possible future action is also discussed.

Written work

1 Writing in role. Give your own account of what happened from the viewpoint of a new character who was a witness to the incident.

2 Play script. Write your own scene of what happens next.

3 Work in pairs to read through your scripts. If you've rehearsed them carefully and feel sufficiently confident you could perform them to the rest of the class.

TRIALS

The classroom becomes a courtroom. A fictional character, historical figure or an organisation is put on trial by the class. Roles such as jury members, judge, witnesses, defence and prosecution counsels may be allocated as required. Verdicts will be decided and appropriate punishment agreed upon, for those found guilty.

Example
Traditional Tales: 'The Big Bad Wolf'

Literacy Links – Year 3 Term 2 Objectives:	T2, 3, 6, 7, 8, 10, S2, S3
PSHE/Citizenship Links:	KS2 2b, f, k

Activities

After reading the story of 'Little Red Riding Hood' the class consider if the wolf is guilty of plotting to eat grandma and Little Red Riding Hood.

Written work

1 Role on the wall. The class fill in an outline of the wolf with adjectives to describe his appearance and behaviour.

2 Shared writing. Opening paragraph for the prosecution when the wolf comes to trial. Why is the wolf guilty?

3 The trial. The classroom furniture is rearranged to resemble a courtroom. With the teacher in role as the judge the children take the role of solicitors. They have to deliver their prepared statements of evidence. The judge decides if they are persuasive enough to convict the wolf of guilt.

LESSONS IN ACTION

A selection of lessons chosen and created by teachers. Many of the lessons offer a sequence of different strategies.

You'll also find examples of written work from children in this section.

Insights

In the drugs awareness day the drama helped to deepen the understanding by stopping it being just story, a cartoon, with the group beginning to realise the impact on mates and family.

Today a class wrote in role, staying in a circle where they'd been doing the drama, and the transition to doing the writing was so natural. After just a few seconds there were no wriggles or shuffles, just complete concentration.

I want the class to revisit the writing they did after the drama yesterday. To look at it more objectively and add to it as they wish. The fifty-word limit I set is intended to be supportive and reassuring for the less able. I'll ask them to read their work to each other in pairs because self-assessment is important, but in role. This will give them an opportunity to respond to what has been read to them about their character. Is it telling of their character? Offensive? True?

Literacy

Traditional Tales: 'The Big Bad Wolf' (5 Lessons)

> **Literacy Links –** (Objectives: T2, 3, 6, 7, 8,10, S2, S3)
> **Year 3 Term 2:** En1 1b, 2c, 4a, b, c, 8a, 10c, 11a; En2
> 2, 3c, 4h, 8f; En3 2, 9a, c, 12
> **PSHE/Citizenship Links:** KS2 2b, f, k

Lesson 1

- Read story of 'Little Red Riding Hood' using finger puppets to illustrate.
- Role on wall – Outline of a wolf face containing negative adjectives to describe his appearance and behaviour.
- Modelling – In pairs, one child as sculptor, the other as model. Model to be positioned as a guilty-looking Big Bad Wolf; create a still picture. Children to describe model's characteristics.
- Explain what a court of law is, including people's roles, i.e. jury, solicitor, court reporter and judge.
- Shared writing – Opening paragraph for prosecution. Why is the wolf guilty of plotting to eat grandma and Little Red Riding Hood?
- Group work – Bulleted lists; evidence from text of wolf's guilt.

Written task (mixed ability pairs)

- Children work in role as solicitors to write persuasively, using evidence from the text to:
  (a) Prosecute – To convince the judge and jury of the Big Bad Wolf's guilt in planning to eat grandma and Little Red Riding Hood.
- Children to have copy of story text and role on wall of wolf adjectives to be displayed on the wall for children to refer to.

Lesson 2

Drama continued

- Space building drama technique. Classroom furniture rearranged to resemble a courtroom.
- Teacher in role as judge. As an alternative a teaching assistant may wish to be in role as judge. Big Bad Wolf in the dock – appropriate costume and props. Set ground rules of drama.
- Children in role as solicitors to deliver their prepared statements of evidence; judge to decide if persuasive enough to convict wolf of guilt.

Lesson 3

- Recap story of Little Red Riding Hood using sequencing drama technique.
- Role on wall – Outline of a wolf containing positive adjectives to describe his appearance and behaviour.
- Modelling – In pairs, one child as sculptor, the other as model. Create a still picture. Model to be positioned as an innocent-looking wolf.
- Shared writing – Opening paragraph for defence. Why is the wolf innocent of plotting to eat grandma and Little Red Riding Hood?
- Group work – Bulleted lists; evidence from text of wolf's innocence. What other reasons could there be for him to be at grandma's house?

Written task (mixed ability pairs)

- Children work in role as the Big Bad Wolf to write persuasively, using evidence from the text to:
  - (b) Defend themselves – To convince the judge and jury of their (the Big Bad Wolf's) innocence in planning to eat grandma and Little Red Riding Hood.
- Children to have copy of story text and role on wall of wolf adjectives to be displayed on the wall for children to refer to.

Lesson 4

Drama continued

- Space building drama technique. Classroom furniture rearranged to resemble a courtroom.
- Teaching assistant in role as judge; teacher in role as court reporter making assessments for speaking and listening – appropriate costume and props. Set ground rules of drama.
- Children in role as the Bid Bad Wolf to deliver their prepared statements of evidence; judge to decide if persuasive enough to be convincing.

Lesson 5

- Personal and peer proof-reading of guilty and innocent statements. How could they be amended to improve them? For example, more convincing adjectives. Amend work.
- Select most convincing argument and independently prepare for class-room display.
- Could be presented in the style of a newspaper report/court reporter's report.

GUILTY

Your honour,

This wolf must instantly go in to jail for the rest of his life. He has carried out three unacceptable crimes. First he locked up a loving, good-natured grandmother in a smelly cupboard with no room to even itch. I don't think this is at all acceptable behaviour. Next he tricked poor Little Red Riding Hood and dressed up as her poor ill grandmother. Then on top of that he doesn't care about anyone or anything but himself. Your honour, if you do not believe me then here is this diary!!!!

INNOCENT

Your honour, I was in forest looking at the breezy trees, when Little Red Riding Hood came along. I told her to pick some colourful flowers for her ill grandma. When I had walked a little way Little Red Riding Hood disappeared. When I got to grandmas cottage, I couldn't find her. Because it was so cold, I had to put on her slippy clothes to get worm. I got into grandmas bed and fell fast asleep. When Little Red Riding Hood came in I was talking in my sleep and I answered her questions. When I was sleep talking. You see, it has all been a big mistake.

Year 6: The Spooky House

Learning Objectives taken from Ros Wilson's *Assessment Criteria Year 6 Planning and Exemplification Units*

Teacher in role

The teacher uses a dual role to introduce the drama.

Firstly wearing a child's baseball cap the teacher takes the role of a ten-year-old who is scared to walk past an old nearby house when its dark. People say the house is haunted. Nobody can see in through the windows of the house and the garden is overgrown with tall trees and brambles.

This strategy creates tension which immediately engages the group and provides a strong starting point.

The teacher then takes off the cap, puts on a tatty old jacket and takes the role of Jack, who lives in the house with his wife Ada. He explains the house has many happy memories for him but that since their children moved away it's become difficult to manage.

It is important to say just a few words in this role leaving many unanswered questions.

Space building

Working in small groups the class recreate rooms or areas in the house as they imagine them. Half the class will be recreating these as imagined by the children of the neighbourhood, the other half as Jack sees them. The group place ordinary objects to represent things or belongings, e.g. a ripped newspaper represents a smashed pane of glass, an upturned hat is a bucket to catch drips from a leaky roof.

The teacher may wish to limit the number of ordinary objects available to each group and to avoid using objects such as tables for safety reasons.

The following plan is a guide for this activity although it may need to be adapted according to numbers in the class.

Imagined by kids

Kitchen
Dining room
Lounge
Back room
Conservatory
Garden

As seen by Jack

Kitchen
Dining room
Lounge
Back room
Conservatory
Garden

Individual writing

After the space building has been completed and the results shared with the whole class, each individual is asked to try and capture the area they created by writing 50 words to describe it.

Time may need to be taken in setting up the writing. An emphasis on the senses is important. Writing should focus on imaginary smells, sounds and sights of the area.

Speaking thoughts

The class sit in a full circle facing outwards. They are invited to speak the thoughts of Jack about the house. They then turn inwards and speak the contrasting thoughts of kids.

This activity is repeated by hearing thoughts from both Jack and the kids about the possible future of the house as contrasting viewpoints.

The teacher may need to support this activity by repeating a few thoughts given in the opening dual role as a demonstration. Further guidance may be offered by hearing a few likely thoughts from able or willing children as a precursor.

Concluding activity

The question that is posed is, 'What will happen to Jack and the house in the future?' Possible scenarios are invited through the creation of a group still picture depicting an imagined future or the class are asked to complete the narrative through a written activity.

An alternative and longer version of this lesson offering a full week's literacy work is to be found on the following pages.

An example of a teacher's working plan

Drama and Literacy Lesson Plan (x1 week – suitable for Years 5 or 6)
Unit: Narrative Writing Suspense Stories – Term 1 or 2

SUSPENSE STORY   Opening ⟶ Build-up (Focus of drama, setting and characters) ⟶
Dilemma (Focus for drama) ⟶ Events ⟶ Resolution and Ending (Focus for drama/writing)

Learning Objectives:

WORD LEVEL	TEXT LEVEL	SENTENCE LEVEL
• Can select from a range of known adventurous vocabulary for a purpose. • Use well-chosen phrases such as adverbials, adventurous and precise vocabulary and other techniques such as sentence variation or figurative language to contribute to the effectiveness of writing.	• Children can up-level their work by developing characters and describe settings, feelings and emotions. • Write with appropriate pace. • In narrative, create characters with some significant interaction between them through direct or reported speech, building characterisation through action, description and characters' responses.	• Can use a wide range of punctuation including full stops, question marks, exclamation marks, commas, apostrophes and inverted commas, usually accurately. • Use the range of different connectives to write coherently.

Objectives taken from: Ros Wilson's Assessment Criteria and Year 6 Planning Exemplification Units

Narrative Writing
Term 1, Units 2 and 5 OR Term 2, Units 2 and 4

	Independent Group Tasks	Plenary	Homework
Class: Year Group(s): Term: Week Beg: Teacher:			
	Drama strategies used: • Teacher in Role (Lesson 1) • Space Building (Lesson 1 and 2) • Freeze Frames (Lesson 3) • Spoken Thoughts (Lesson 3 and 4)		
Mon • Teacher in role as Stacey and then Mr. Smith with different viewpoints of the cottage – set the scene.	• In groups of 4 or 5 label groups (Mr. Smith or Stacey). • Create one room in the cottage through the eyes of their characters (space building). • On clipboards describe the scene in 50 words in character/ role as Mr. Smith or Stacey.	• Read out the descriptions of the house through the eyes of their characters.	
Tues • Recap previous lesson – Drama and writing. Children look at writing from previous session and re-draft, paying close attention to: adventurous vocabulary, wide range of punctuation and sentence openers.	• Write up descriptions of the cottage in role as characters on writing frame.	• Re-read descriptions of the house and discuss editing process.	

An example of a teacher's working plan (*continued*)

Wed	• Move story forward. Stacey and friends go to cottage at night. Stacey dared to go in by friends. Stacey is terrified – remembers stories about witches and ghosts etc. Mr. Smith inside house, hears noises, goes to investigate, kids or visitors?	• In same groups as Monday (4 or 5 children), create a freeze frame of the moment. Stacey goes to the front door – Mr. Smith behind door.	• Go over suspense writing elements. • Focus on 'build up': –short sentences – ellipsis … – empty words: 'someone', 'something' etc.
Thu	• Recap previous lesson – 'freeze frames' (as Stacey goes to front door and opens it slowly and sees …). • Recap features of a suspense story like a roller coaster ride (build up – end) etc.	• Show freeze frames – add spoken thoughts. • Writing – 50 words, write how Stacey felt when she goes to front door and opens door (build up) – short sentences etc. • Use empty words to describe the 'thing' she sees behind the door. • Write up descriptions of the build up on writing frame.	• Recap different parts of a suspense story and focus for tomorrow: – dilemma and resolution etc.
Fri	• Recap previous lesson – 'writing and drama'. Revise structure of a suspense story. Focus on dilemma: – Stacey's: Should she go in? What will she find? – Mr Smith's: Should he investigate noises etc? and discuss what happens next in the story (events and resolution/ending)	• Children decide after discussion how their stories will develop, what happens next (events) and how the story will end or be resolved. *Draft, edit and write in best.	• Review all the drama process and writing structure for a suspense story. • Read what happens next and endings.

An example of a teacher's working plan (*continued*)

Space building:
creating an imaginary room

Writing 50 words to describe the room

Writing 50 words to say
how Stacey felt

One of the plenary sessions:
suspense writing elements

Using freeze frames to recap

Freeze frame between
Mr Smith and Stacey

Written work from a Year 5 boy:
The Haunted House

Every day I walk past the haunted and spooky looking place. So I decided to step in through the gap in the hedge with my mate Cody to see if it really is haunted.

We walked into the abandoned garden and all you could smell was fish, mould and more fish. The state of the place was horrendous. The first thing we saw was an armless teddy bear with mould coming out of one its eyes. If you think this is bad it isn't the half of it.

There were dead birds, a key, rusted old doors and disturbingly mouldy old chairs. We carried on but we wanted to back off because the state of the place gave us horrible feelings.

We were both shivering. All I could hear in my head was 'Don't go any further, it will be horrible and scary.' But on we went. We came to the creaky door of the house and I put my hand on the cold, gold and smooth door handle...

... and the Clock Struck Thirteen ...

Objective: To understand how the use of descriptive language can be used to create moods and build tension.

NC Refs:	1.4, 1.11, 3.1b, 3.1c, 3.1d, 3.2a, 3.9a

Prior to drama lesson

Begin reading *Tom's Midnight Garden* by Philippa Pearce (Puffin).

Drama activity

Children lie on the floor pretending to be in bed. Re-read page 19 of *Tom's Midnight Garden* about the clock striking 13.

(Ring a bell or children create the sound effects of a grandfather clock slowly chiming 13 times)

Either read the beginning of Chapter 3 where Tom gets out of bed, or talk the children through this process, asking them to sit up in bed and creep downstairs. The children need to be absolutely silent as they must not wake Uncle Alan, Aunt Gwen or especially old Mrs Bartholomew.

Build up the tension and freeze-frame

(If possible have the sound effect of a slow and steady tick, tick, tick ... quietly in the background)

Discuss how Tom was feeling – tension, anxiety, excitement, heart pounding, pulse raising, palms sweating etc. Share these ideas and record.

Music

To capture the feeling of tension/suspense through sound. Each child needs an instrument (triangle, maraca, bells, wood block, tambour etc.). Begin with one child quietly playing their instrument, point to the second child, the third and so on to join in. Gradually build up the music and the tension, before encouraging the sound effect to slow down and fade away one child at a time again.

Writing

What happens to Tom next/what does he discover?

The children continue with the story, creating their own version of why the clock struck 13.

> When the clock strikes thirteen
>
> Tom stopped... the door was chained... the clock handle had rusted off... what should he do? Go back to bed? Or find a way to find the time without waking Uncle Alan or Aunt Gwen. Suddenly the moon shone through the stained red window (on the door) like fire and it was true... the clock had Struck... 13 o'clock. And then the old garther clocks back... opened. Tom crept round to the back there was a.... door just big enough for Tom and he unlocked it using skill.
>
> He stepped in slowly... slowly shutting his eyes thinking something bad would happen, but no, he felt a crunching at his feet as though stepping on freshly cut grass. Wait a second it was freshly cut grass. He opened his eyes thinking it would wake him up, but no, it was real, every bit of it from the grass to the smell wait a second what was that smell? It smelt like a mixture of Blue-bells, White-bells and Daffodils wait a minute it was. And what was that noise? It was an owl hooting with joy before ripping its prey apart and feeding it to soft, slimy infants waiting to grow in to adults and then hunt down small creatures. Ouch! What was that spiky which met my slipperless feet 3.5 seconds ago? So what was I in ... a secret garden which belongs to... me.

The Key

Objective: To write a story with a focus from the N.C. level descriptors:

Level 3:	Encourage writing which is structured, imaginative and clear.
Level 4:	Sustained ideas should be developed interestingly and organised effectively to reader's purpose.

Drama activity

Ask children to close eyes and create a mind picture while teacher talks through a morning's events. Tell pupils to imagine they are waking up in the morning. Ask them to think about several questions, for example, what day of the week is it? Is the sun shining? What time of year is it?

Ask the children to open their eyes and drop a letter on the floor. Tell them to imagine it is addressed to them and it has just been posted through their letter box. Open the envelope or ask a child to slowly open the envelope to reveal an old, large key.

Share ideas about where the key has come from, why it has been sent to you and what it is for. Play quiet music in the background while pupils close their eyes and think about the events of their story. Ask the children if anyone has a clear idea of events in their mind and if they would like to be hot seated.

Choose a child to be hot seated. Pupils ask questions about who they are, what age they are and who they think could have sent the key. Several children have a turn in the hot seat.

Children return to their seats and take part in brain-gym activities (lazy 8s and other cross-lateral activities). Remind children of their objective before starting writing.

The Three Little Pigs (with a difference)

Objectives: To take notes.

To create a newspaper report based on the evidence given by Mr Wolf and Mr Pig.

NC Refs
English: 1.2b, 1.2c,1 .4, 3.1a, 3.1c
ICT: 2a

Lesson introduction

Tell or read the 'Three Little Pigs' to the children and explain that this is a real scenario as told by Mr Pig.

Then read *The True Story of the Three Little Pigs* by Jon Scieszka (ISBN 0 -14-054056-3). This is an account from Mr Wolf's point of view explaining how he visited Mr Pig, his neighbour, simply to borrow a cup of sugar to make his dear old granny a birthday cake!

Drama activity

Arrange the classroom for a press conference. Seating should be facing the front where a table and chair will be placed to interview Mr Wolf and Mr Pig. The teacher will be in role as these characters and should have an appropriate prop such as a mask to portray the pig and wolf realistically.

Identify and discuss the objective of the lesson with the class. Pupils will be newspaper reporters and take notes from the accounts given by Mr Wolf and Mr Pig. They will later have to use their notes to create a newspaper report about the incident.

Mr Pig is introduced to the press conference and hot seated by the children in role as reporters. Quotes are taken from Mr Pig and notes made.

Mr Wolf is interviewed next. He explains that his reputation of being 'big and bad' is unfounded, he has been misunderstood and just wanted to borrow a cup of sugar from his neighbours, the three little pigs. He had a terrible cold at the time and his sneezes were mistaken for 'huffing and puffing'. Had the piglets chosen better building material for their houses then perhaps his sneezes would not have blown their buildings down.

Writing activity

Pupils use their notes to create a newspaper article representing the facts as told by Mr Pig and Mr Wolf. They should be encouraged to use quotes and write in report style. The finished report can be presented as a newspaper article using ICT.

Examples of children's work

The Real Story of the Big Bad Wolf

It all began when I was walking through the dark and very muddy forest. I had just got about half way through the forest when a shadow appeared from the darkness! I was sure I heard it growl, but then maybe not. Soon is began, very, very slowly to come closer and closer. When it was about ten metres away it started belching towards me! I started to back away. I stopped. Where was the wolf? Suddenly I heard a very faint growling coming from behind me. Behind me was a shaggy wolf. It looked at me and cocked his head to one side. Suddenly ... he began to itch like mad!

After a surprisingly, ginourmousely, humungously 8 massive hours, when the wolf had stopped scratching, I bent down and then he ... licked me on the hand! I wonder where you came from? No idea! Said the wolf. I was so A-B-S-O-L-U-T-L-Y shocked to hear him answer me! I tried telling him a joke. Which author writes books for little bees? Easy pezzy lemon squeezy. Said the wolf.

I put a rope round the wolfs neck and gave it to my cousin Jack because it was his birthday. When Jack was playing with his wolf the wolf got angry with Jack and gobbled him up.

The True Story About the Wolf

The forest was dark and gloomy and the sun never came out. I know I'm scared because people go in and never come out …

… Deep in a clearing there lay a cottage. By the cottage Mr Wolf and his children played. One playing basketball the other playing hop scotch and Mr Wolf was reading the paper.

One morning Mr Wolf said, 'Good morning my darling I am just going to chop some wood,' and off he went. But he got carried off the path to a cottage. He knocked on the door …

… An old woman opened the door. The wolf noticed the woman's teeth were huge. Mr Wolf said exactly that. The women said, 'All the better to eat you with!' The woman lunged . The wolf could not bare to be eaten. He opened his mouth and the woman landed in his mouth.

So that is how the wolf got the blame.

Year 8: Poetry of the First World War

Focus: *Dulce et Decorum Est* – Wilfrid Owen

Literacy Links:	Word Level Y9.7 (layers of meaning in writer's choice of words); Sentence Level Y9.5 (evaluate their ability to shape ideas rapidly ...); Text Level Y9.11 (make telling use of descriptive detail)

Preparation

The teacher reads the poem through (A3 copy) for the class, then asks them to read it through individually. Pairs text-marked as follows:

- words which suggest tiredness;
- words which suggest disgust;
- words which suggest the writer's helplessness.

The class then reported back and a brief discussion followed to consolidate understanding of the narrative and the poet's viewpoint.

Drama

- Still frame: choose a moment in the poem. Rest of the class look at one group at a time to suggest:
  - adjectives to describe the quality/feeling of the moment (scribe on whiteboard);
  - what the body language tells us of the life they had.
  Thought tracking what their feelings and attitudes are.
- Speaking thoughts: class in a circle, stepping forward to say which character they are, what their thoughts/feelings are about the incident. (Requires teacher modelling for inexperienced group.)

- Space building: class imagines they are visitors to the scene later; place a significant object in the centre of the circle, describe it briefly.

Writing

Immediately ... write 50 words to describe the scene, the event, people's reactions.

An example of Year 8 work

A faint scream interrupted the empty silence. My vision was beginning to blur, I tripped and fell helplessly to the ground. Was there any point in getting up? Pain infected my tiresome body, but somehow I mustered up some strength and managed to get up. Trudging on, I looked up at the sky as if to say, 'help me.' Help did not come. Instead, something much less welcoming arrived ... gas bombs! All around me my companions dropped down like dominoes. I heard another scream, but this time it was closer ... it was my scream. The poison had struck, but I didn't quite give up. Getting weaker and weaker, I attempted to run for cover. Stumbling and falling, stumbling and falling, stumbling and falling ... gone.

Year 8: Poetry of the First World War

Focus: *Christmas 1924* – Thomas Hardy

> **Literacy Links:** W8.13 (ironic use of words); R8.6 (bias and objectivity); R8.7 (implied meaning); Wr9.13 (influence audience); Wr9.14 (counter argument); S and L 9.12 (work in role)

Preparation

- A4 copies of poem.
- Dictionaries.
- Read poem with class.
- Find definition of irony.
- Text-mark poem, using highlighters and making notes on ideas suggested by words, meaning of poem. (May need teacher modelling, e.g. 'Peace upon earth' reminds me of the words of a Christmas carol, which we sing at Christmas, but also makes me think of peace after war, so I'm going to highlight that and write …')
- Discuss the irony – the difference between what the poet says in the poem and what he actually means/feels.

Drama

- Teacher in role: as Thomas Hardy; first establish what kind of questions we'd asked, e.g. why he wrote the poem, what does he mean by …?
- Hot seating: pupils in fours with one offering to be an indignant retired colonel who objects to the poem.

Writing

- Letter to a newspaper: pupils imagine the poem has been published in *The Times*; write to the editor either in support of Hardy's views or in opposition. Factors to consider: voice; persuasive language – connectives, use of a question, emotive vocabulary etc.; counter-argument.

Christmas 1924: Extracts of written work by children

Sir

Last weekend I was happily reading my newspaper in full Christmas spirit when I stumbled across the revolting poem by Thomas Hardy.

I have always respected and enjoyed Mr Hardy's work. Now I see him and his writing in a completely different light and can no longer appreciate it....courageous men died for their country including both of our dear sons....But now Mr Hardy is saying they died for absolutely nothing. No mother wants to hear that their son died for nothing let alone have it printed in their weekly paper and I have no words for how despicable I believe that is !

Sir

I am writing to you about the poem published last week in The Times by Thomas Hardy. I just wanted to share a few of my thoughts about it with the readers. I think it is a splendid poem about war...

The question I want to raise is' why?' Why hasn't God helped the suffering and dying ? Why hasn't praying and praying helped anyone ? I feel betrayed...

Sir

I regret to inform you of an outrageous poem in your newspaper...

Firstly, I feel strongly about the war and proud to have been fighting for my country, unlike the writer of this poem who knows nothing about what men went through during four years of torture...I am a religious man and believe in God....

Focus: *Goodnight Mr Tom* – Michelle Magorian

Literacy Links:	W Y7.14 (deploy words with precision); S variety – 7.1; 7.2 and 8.1; 8.2; 8.3; T Wr. 7.1 (plan, edit etc.); 8.2 (re-read ... effect on reader ...); 7.6 (portray character ...); 7.9 (links between reading and their choices as writers); 7.14 (describe a person ...)

Preparation

- Read Chapter 1 of *Goodnight Mr Tom* by Michelle Magorian (Puffin).

Drama

- Still frame: fours choose one scene/incident in Chapter 1. Selected groups freeze while the rest of the class add adjectives to describe the mood/feelings of the characters or the atmosphere of the scene, think of captions to capture the moment, discuss what the body language tells the audience. Scribe on flip chart. Characters in the scene voice their thoughts when touched on shoulder.

- Modelling: pairs model Mr Tom and Willie. Add adjectives/phrases and thought tracking. Scribe useful vocabulary on flipchart.

- Role on the wall: halve the class, one half as Willie, one half as Mr Tom. Outline a body and use different coloured pens to write words within the outline about how Mr Tom/Willie view themselves – characteristics, possibly possessions. Swap groups and write how the other character views from outside the outline. Look at and discuss ideas.

- Writing: individually, write a short description of one of the characters.

Focus: *Goodnight Mr Tom* – Michelle Magorian

Literacy Links:	Text Level Writing: 7.1 (plan, draft etc.); Y8.2 (effect on reader); Y7.14 (describe ... using language effectively ...)

Preparation

- Class will need to have read at least to Chapter 5.

Drama

- Explain that we are going to write the *Little Weirwold Observer's* report on the arrival of the evacuees.

- Who would the reporters want to interview? Fours draw up a list, share with class. Consider points of view of evacuees and villagers, problems and positive aspects.

- Allocate one of suggested situations and characters to each group. They role plan an incident and have to be prepared to freeze frame a key moment. Thought track the characters. Write/suggest a caption/headline as if this were a photo in the newspaper.

- Forum theatre: move the group role plays into a film with children sitting out to watch as reporters. They can stop action, add new developments, advise characters, discuss different approaches and conduct interviews.

- Groups decide which article (point of view/character's experience) they are going to write together. Ensure even spread of bias. Groups write and edit.

An example of Year 7 writing

Zak

His curly, ginger hair makes him look like a girl and his sparklin' blue eyes shimmer in the moonlight. The cheekiness of him is quite rude yet he seems to be just too over polite. I wish he wouldn't be as abrupt as that, Mr. Tom looks like he'll bite back any second! I do hope Mr. Tom don't hurt me or give me a beatin', I've had many of those in me life and now I'm scared stiff. What if he gives Zak a beatin'; he's such a wicked boy bein' all rude like that ... I bet he gets lots of beatin's from his parents.

PSHE

Stealing

PSHE and Citizenship Objectives:	KS2 2b, d, 4a.
Literacy Links:	KS2 En1 2b, c, 3a, b, c, f, 4a, c, 11a; En3 12.

1. Narration

The teacher gives a short introduction describing how Billy and his friends go into a local sweet shop. Billy is nine years old and hasn't stolen before but he feels the pressure of friends to do so. The shopkeeper is a friend of Billy's family.

2. Conscience alley

Should Billy steal or not? Ask one of the class to take the role of Billy. Represent the conflicting pressures upon him of his friend and that of his own conscience. Ask Billy to indicate which pressure is the stronger by moving to that part of the alley at the conclusion of the strategy.

3. Narration

Whatever decision Billy takes in the conscience alley he is now under even more pressure from mates. He goes into the shop with a friend and steals, with the friend as a decoy.

4. Still image

Imagine the scene described in the narration has been videoed by a hidden security camera. Work in a group of three (Billy, friend and shop-keeper) to recreate the scene which the video has captured. Try to concentrate on the moment of Billy stealing, which appears to be undetected at that time.

5. Thought track

Ask all groups to take still positions at the moment of stealing and thought track the participants. The thoughts expressed should then be written down.

6. Narration

The shopkeeper later checks the video, sees Billy stealing and visits Billy's house to break the news to one of his parents.

7. Forum theatre

Parent confronts Billy in an angry way. Does Billy tell the truth about the stealing? Rerun the scene several times with Billy and parent taking a range of contrasting attitudes and exchanging roles in turn with different class members. Which attitudes bring the most helpful outcome?

8. Small group playmaking

Run a scene as above but now add a punishment that the parent has decided upon. Discuss.

9. Speaking thoughts

Put yourself in the position of the shopkeeper. Speak thoughts of your final attitude towards Billy as he visits the shop again.

Written work

Return to the thoughts which have been written down earlier. Using this as a basis and working as a whole group undertake collaborative writing in the form of a playscript to capture one of the shoplifting scenes. Include what is thought but not spoken as well as what is actually said. Write other scenes individually.

Bullying

Objective: To recognise that actions can affect ourselves and others, to consider the feelings of others, and attempt to perceive their point of view.

NC Refs	
PSHE:	4a, 4d, 4g
	Eng 1.9a, 1.11a, 2.5b, 2.5f, 2.5g

Introduction

Put the question 'What is a bully?' to the children and discuss their answers. Ask the children if bullies usually act alone or when they have an 'audience'/other children who will join in with them or encourage them.

Drama activity 1

Organise the pupils into groups of five or six. Each group will have a long sheet of paper on the floor on which to draw round one of its members. Ask the children to think of adjectives to describe the emotions of a child being bullied. These should be written on the inside of the shape, adjectives to describe the bully should be placed outside the shape. Share each group's work with the class and consider people's choice of language for each characteristic.

Drama activity 2

Ask the children to sit on chairs arranged in a circle. Explain to the children that you will leave the room and when you return, you will be a parent whose child has been bullied by a group of pupils in school.

Use cap or jacket when you go into role as parent to distinguish fiction and reality.

Return to the class out of role, as the teacher, and ask the children how this activity made them feel.

Continue the story by explaining that Amy hasn't gone home at the end of the day. Her parents are very worried and have alerted the police. Now the children in Amy's class have to face the possibility that she may have run away because she was being bullied.

Drama activity 3

Ask the children to remain in their chairs but turn them so they are facing outwards. Pupils take the role of the bullies who are feeling worried/ashamed about the way Amy has been treated. Ask the children to take it in turns round the circle to either express their feelings of guilt or worry or say why they bullied Amy.

Writing activity 1

Ask the children to move from their chairs to a different area (they may have been sitting still for a while). Tell the children that thankfully, Amy was found safe and sound. She had been hiding in her grandparents' holiday cottage, and is now beginning to feel better after discussing her problems with her parents. The school know about the bullying and have spoken with the pupils involved. Amy will be returning to school next week.

Ask the children if they can become involved in ensuring that the bullying doesn't happen again. Ask them to work in pairs to think about:

1 What they should do if they see someone being bullied.
2 What is the best way to react if someone is bullying you?

Writing/art activity 2

Using the previous activity discuss how the ideas can be condensed into short, thought-provoking statements suitable for a poster.

Don't allow the lesson to spiral into negative personal accounts of being bullied. Reinforce the positive, encouraging children to think about their good qualities and that it is 'OK' to be different.

Make bold, clear posters to help stop bullying and to remind children what they should do if they are being bullied.

History

The Second World War: The Blitz

History Links:	KS2 4a, b, 5c, 8a, 11b
Literacy Links:	En1 2a, 4a, b, c, 11a. Enc3 1a, 9a, 10, 11

To set the scene

Hall in a mess as if the aftermath of a bombing raid.

Children enter, but no mention is as yet made regarding the scene. Children sit in a circle.

Explain to the children that this is no longer the school hall, but for the time that we are going to be working in here, it will be a street.

Explain that at times during the drama, both yourself and the children will take on roles of other people, but that you will tell them who and when.

Suggest a start and stop signal to clearly show when the drama is taking place, e.g. when I turn around and sit down I will be ....

Tell the children that when you go into the centre of the circle you will become a character that lives in this street, and that their job is to find out about the character by asking questions. They are to take it in turns, they may ask a question when they are holding the object, but they must all listen carefully to the answers to find out as much as possible.

Teacher in role as a child who is experiencing air raids. Take a gas mask as a prop.

Hot seating to take place.

The teacher in role explains about the sound of the air raid siren. Tell the children that next time they hear the siren they will go back in time and be other children from her family at the time of one of these raids. They must listen very carefully to find out what to do.

When they hear the sound of the siren they must imagine themselves as a child, frightened, worried, not sure what to do. When the siren stops, they need to freeze in a pose to show how the children would possibly feel. Still picture to take place. (This could be as individuals, or twos or threes.)

Remaining still, if touched on their shoulder, the children must then say how they are feeling, any thoughts that they have etc. Thought tracking takes place.

Out of role they are then asked to come back and sit in the circle. Teacher in role then talks to the children about one particular night when she had a problem, just as an air raid began. 'Hot seat' to find out about the missing brother and how she was feeling etc. Teacher explains dilemma – should she go and look for her brother, or look after her own life and go into the shelter?

Conscience alley

Explain to the children that they need to help her decide what to do next – split the children into two groups: one to try and convince her to go and look for him and why, the other telling her of the dangers and not to go as time is short. Split the children from both sides into pairs to allow them a minute's thinking time of what they are going to say as their argument. Teacher in role then goes down the 'alley' listening to their points of view – what did she decide? (Went to find brother, and got into the shelter just in time!)

Teacher back in role

Explain to the children that they then went into the shelter – hot seat questions as to what it was like in the shelter.

Explain out of role that at the end of an air raid an all clear siren was sounded, but that when people emerged they did not know what they were going to find, and whether or not there had been any strikes nearby. Explain that they are all going to go back into role, and be in the shelter, and that after the signal they will come out, and view the devastation in the hall – the remains of where houses had been.

Children in role

Listen to all clear signal and come out of shelter to look at the mess. Encourage the children to talk to each other in role about what they have found. Encourage them to use their senses to describe what they could hear, see, smell and taste as well as how they felt. In small groups the children could brainstorm these ideas and jot them onto a large piece of paper, only give short time to do this and then share together.

Still picture

In small groups the children then compose a picture to show the shock of seeing the destruction caused. How can they convey the anguish, sadness, misery, fear etc.? Take real photos of their tableaux using the digital camera for use later on in class. The children then compose a caption to go with their picture and write it on a large piece of paper, placing it in front of themselves.

If time, thought tracking could take place, choosing one or two individuals from each group.

Follow-up writing activities

- Diary extract from a child's point of view telling of their experiences.
- Newspaper article – use the photo taken as a starting point, add headline and report using interviews with people who were there.
- A letter from a child who experienced the raids to a child who had been evacuated to the country.
- Poetry, based on the senses to describe the air raid experience.

An example of written work

After the Air Raid.........

As soon as I stepped out of the shelter there was a hush all around. I couldn't see a thing because of all the smoke. Suddenly I heard clear footsteps on the ragged street. I stood there relieved to be alive until it cleared. My next door neighbours roof was crashed on the garden floor. I could still see the red hot flames creeping down the street. There were flickers of ash going past my face. There were smells of acid, poison and gas. My sight was clearing, but I thought I was blind. But no, I could still see planes on the horizon. I thought I was mistaken, but how many swear words I could hear being spoken. I could even taste the gas, poison and acid. I saw people wanting to go into their houses, but others were stopping them. I wasn't afraid. I went in and the door creaked and the floor cracked. Mum came in and took control by taking me back out. As we turned round the corner we saw our gran had died. Mum was so sad, her eyes were like waterfalls. My brother followed us, crying with his broken teddy.

The Second World War: History/Literacy/Music

Objectives:

- To understand and explore in greater depth the impact of the Second World War on children.
- To write a diary account.
- To write an informal letter.

NC Refs	
History:	2.a, 2c, 5c, 11b
English:	1.1, 1.3, 1.4, 3.1, 3.2
Music:	1a, 1c, 3b

Prior to drama

Pupils make gas mask boxes to wear around neck and papier mâché tin helmets using balloons as mould and a cardboard rim measured to fit head. Paint khaki green.

Children learn to sing 'Pack up your troubles in your old kit bag' and 'It's a long way to Tipperary'. These harmonise well together and can be sung as a round.

Drama activity 1

Set the scene of a railway station in 1930s Britain. Draw a line on the hall floor with chalk to indicate where the train arrives, with benches or chairs behind the line to represent the seats in the train. Children wear their tin hats and carry a rucksack.

Explain to the children that they will be young men leaving their wives and children to go to war.

Represent the arrival of the train at the station by blowing a whistle. The children pick up their belongings and clamber onto the train. They sit on the benches and begin to sing the round – 'It's a long way...' and 'Pack up...'.

An alternative to the above would be for half the class to be the young men and the other half to be their families standing on the platform. The soldiers would sing 'Pack up your troubles' and the family members sing 'It's a long way to Tipperary'.

Discuss with the children the emotions that would have been experienced by the soldiers and their families. Brainstorm for adjectives and adjectival phrases. Improve and develop together using a flip chart/OHP or tablet PC. Save this work for follow up writing.

Writing task

Children write a diary extract expressing their feelings about their fathers going to war.

Drama activity 2

The children are evacuees waiting at the railway station with gas mask boxes round their necks and carrying their favourite teddy bear. Signal the arrival of the train with a whistle. Children mime hugging their parents goodbye. Freeze frame.

This is followed by children working in groups of three or four. One child is modelled by their peers who physically move his/her body into a position which shows them leaning out of the train window and waving goodbye. Encourage the children modelling to ask the child being modelled to apply facial expression to the character for effect.

Writing task

Children write a letter home to inform parents of their arrival and how they are feeling.

Alternative writing activities: a play script or a second diary extract.

The Evacuee

One sad winters afternoon, in the middle of the cold, damp, smoky train station, Lucy Elderwood stood bolt upright with her boxed gasmask hanging around her neck. In one hand she cluched a small brown teddy-bear and a little suit-case in the other. As she was bundled into a train carriage she sadly waved at her mother until the station disappeared out of sight. Lucy stared out of the window as the cities became contry side After a long trip, the trian slowed down then screeched to a halt. The children rushed out of the train, Lucy followed anxiously, to she hadnt a clue where her new hom would be.

Second World War – additional material

Extract of a fictional diary written by a teacher. The class are asked to imagine that this has been written by an evacuee. The letter is unfinished and needs pupil initiative in writing and drama for further exploration.

Diary

Thursday 18th March

I can't believe that I'm here surrounded by a hundred other children and yet I feel so alone. Mother has gone but I can still smell her perfume on the collar of my coat. I mustn't cry. My baby brother Peter is curled up asleep next to me. I've got to be strong for him. And for me.

There's strangers all around us. We're all ....

The central image of the brother and sister evacuees was projected onto a white board. Working as a whole class collaboratively the teacher scribed the children's words to describe the feelings of both characters. Individual hard copies of the photograph were then handed out for a similar process to occur but now as a solo activity.

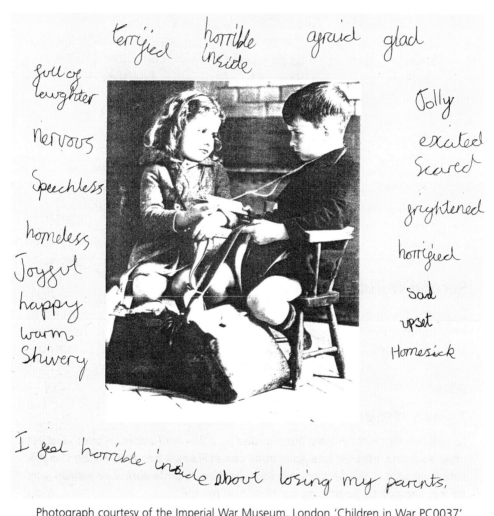

Photograph courtesy of the Imperial War Museum, London 'Children in War PC0037'

Having also discussed the diary extract on the previous page the children are now ready to write their own fictional diaries describing the feelings and emotions of being an evacuee.

Write the speech bubbles.

Photograph courtesy of the Imperial War Museum, London 'Childrn in War PC0037'.

Photograph 1

RE

The Christmas Story

Objectives:

- To understand why Mary and Joseph had to travel to Bethlehem.
- To understand the significance of the shepherds, the wise men and Herod with the birth of Jesus.

This series of lessons consist of a whole day's activities, or alternatively could take place over several days.

Introduction

Familiarise children with the Christmas story through reading/telling the story and using visual aids.

Drama and writing activity 1

Play a relevant Christmas carol such as 'How far is it to Bethlehem?', 'O little town of Bethlehem' or 'Little donkey' in the background. Discuss with the children about Mary and Joseph's journey to Bethlehem. Why were they travelling there? Where is Bethlehem?

Children work in small groups to discuss the emotions/feelings that might have been experienced by Mary and Joseph – 'tiredness, excitement, fear' etc. Provide children with large pre-drawn silhouettes of Mary riding a donkey. Fit their adjectives/adjectival phrases within the silhouette to create a role on the wall of feelings.

Drama activity 2

How did Mary and Joseph feel when they arrived in Bethlehem and there were no rooms left in the town? Create a forum theatre with the teacher in role as the innkeeper and two children in role as Mary and Joseph.

Joseph knocks on the inn door, he and Mary try to persuade the inn keeper to let them stay for the night. (At this point the innkeeper does not let them in.)

Teacher stops the roleplay and asks the class how Joseph and Mary could be more persuasive.

Other children take the roles to replace the first Mary and Joseph. Eventually the innkeeper opens the door and offers Mary and Joseph his stable.

An alternative to the above drama activity would be for children to work in groups of three and all roleplay Mary, Joseph and the innkeeper.

Drama activity 3

Space building: in small groups, the children create the stable where Jesus was born using resources available in the classroom/hall. For example, a classroom book tray could be the manger and a school jumper, baby Jesus. Pupils take it in turns to discuss their created space to the other groups and explain what their items represent.

Children should be encouraged to use expressive language and to describe how the stable looks, smells and feels.

Drama activity 4

The shepherds: tell or read the story of the shepherds watching their flocks at night on a hillside. Discuss what it may have been like to be a shepherd 2000 years ago.

If a planetarium is available for school visits in your area you may find it useful to contact them.

The children lie down as if they are watching the night sky. A Chrismas carol such as 'While shepherds watched their flocks by night' may be used as background music. Pupils call out their feelings – 'dark, cold, wolves about, lonely' etc.

Pupils take the role of shepherds in groups of three or four. The arrival of the Angel Gabriel is signalled by the teacher. At this point, the children look towards a pre-chosen spot on the wall which signifies where Gabriel appears; they cover their faces/gasp etc. Freeze frame.

Children take it in turns to look at each other's freeze frames and write a caption, for example 'Blinded by the light', 'An angel of the Lord appears on a hillside'. These captions may be used as newspaper headlines.

Writing activity

Newspaper report about the Angel Gabriel appearing to the shepherds and informing them about the 'Good News'.

Drama activity 5

Tell or read the story of the Wise Men and Herod. Discuss with children the reasons for Herod's reaction to the news of Jesus' birth.

Arrange the chairs (including the teacher's chair) in a circle. All children stand behind their chairs, moving along one place at a time. As each child reaches the teacher's chair, they speak out (single word or short phrase) to tell Herod what their opinion of him is.

Possible writing activities

- A letter to warn Mary and Joseph about Herod's intention to kill Jesus.
- Character portrait of King Herod.
- Work in pairs to create a play script of the whole Christmas story, each child writing two scenes.
- A diary extract by one of the Wise Men giving an account of his arrival at the stable in Bethlehem.

Glossary

Caption A title or heading that accompanies another piece of work such as a still image.

Ceremony Special event created to mark or celebrate something significant.

Collaborative writing With an adult as scribe and arbiter the whole group work together to produce one piece of writing made up of different individual ideas, words and sentences.

Conscience alley Standing in two facing rows, pros and cons are put forward as a character walks down the alley and listens to the conflicting advice given.

Costume or prop Articles of costume or special objects presented as an introduction to a culture or lifestyle of a character or place.

Dream pictures Drawings and phrases to depict a dream which a fictional character may have had.

Forum theatre A drama interaction of two or more characters is interrupted allowing time out to be given where advice is fed back to one or both of the characters. The interaction is then rerun taking on board advice given.

Hot seating A character is put on the spot and questioned by the rest of the group. Answers are given in role by the character.

In role Taking the part of someone other than yourself in the drama.

Journeys An adult leads the group through different parts of the building or site as if they are exploring an imaginative land or country.

Meetings Gathering together in role to discuss an issue or problem.

Mime Using body movement and gestures, without words, to express an idea, show an action or portray a character.

Modelling Creating a statue or frozen character by moving your body into an appropriate position.

Movement sequences Using movements, improvised or rehearsed, to explore a situation, place, feeling or event.

Narrate To tell a story or set a scene.

Role on the wall Filling in a drawn outline of a character with words or phrases which describe that character.

Sequencing An active and practical way to create a time line or the order of scenes in a play by using people to make the line.

Sound collage Use voices, objects and instruments to create a sound picture of a place, mood, theme or story.

Space building Create an imaginary space, building or environment by placing everyday objects to represent significant things within the space.

Speaking thoughts Children speak the thoughts of characters.

Still image Using the body to create a frozen picture.

Teacher in role The teacher takes the part of a fictional character in the drama.

Thought tracking Children speak aloud the feelings and emotions of a character while participating in a still image depiction of that character.

Trial The classroom becomes a courtroom where a fictional character is put on trial by the class.

Bibliography

Ackroyd, J. (2000) *Literacy Alive: Drama Projects for Literacy Learning.* Hodder Murray.

Carter, D. (2000) *Teaching Fiction in the Primary School.* David Fulton.

Corbett, P. (2002) *How to Teach Fiction Writing at Key Stage 2.* David Fulton.

Grudgeon, E. and Gardner, P. (2001) *The Art of Storytelling for Teachers and Pupils: Using Stories to Develop Literacy in Primary Classrooms.* David Fulton.

Kempe, A. and Holroyd, J. (2004) *Speaking, Listening and Drama.* David Fulton.

Kempe, A. and Lockwood, M. (2000) *Drama In and Out of the Literacy Hour.* University of Reading.

Lamont, G. et al. (2000) *100 Ideas For Drama.* Collins Educational.

Neelands, J. (1990) *Structuring Drama Work.* Cambridge University Press.

Neelands, J. (2004) *Beginning Drama 11–14.* David Fulton.

Palmer, S. (2000) *How to Teach Writing across the Curriculum at Key Stage 2.* David Fulton.

Other resources

BBC Video Plus Pack/Zig Zag (2002) *Children and the 2nd World War.*

Department for Education and Skills (2003) Primary National Strategy. *Speaking, Listening and Learning: Working with Children in Key Stages 1 and 2.*

The box of materials includes a helpful video of classroom examples. If you're unsure of how drama strategies work in practice the video will provide you with practical demonstrations.

The Imperial War Museum Education Department has a whole host of excellent resources for supporting work in schools, especially First and Second World War material. This includes replica artefacts such as gas masks (original gas masks are highly toxic and contain asbestos), posters and evocative evacuee photographs. A comprehensive catalogue is available.

Build up your own collection of original artefacts as stimulus for drama and writing. Old keys, hats, gloves, shoes, photographs, postcards etc. can be the starting point for character and narrative exploration.

Use visits to historical sites, unusual buildings, museums as stimulus. Pose questions to discover hidden stories. Invent scenarios. Use still images back in school to begin to build ideas. Give children opportunity to produce their own versions of the past and present.

Index